LEMURS

LIVING WILD

Published by Creative Education and Creative Paperbacks
P.O. Box 227, Mankato, Minnesota 56002
Creative Education and Creative Paperbacks are imprints of The Creative Company
www.thecreativecompany.us

Design and production by Mary Herrmann
Art direction by Rita Marshall
Printed in China

Photographs by Alamy (AF archive, Arco Images GmbH, Ariadne Van Zandbergen), Creative Commons Wikimedia (Twowells/Ölands Djurpark, Frank Vassen/Attis1979/Flickr, Rod Waddington/Flickr), Dreamstime (Anolis01, Lukas Blazek, Hang61922595, Heartjump, Javarman, Rico Leffanta, Gilles Malo, Smellme), iStockphoto (Goddard_Photography), Shutterstock (Bob Ascott, BGSmith, Ryan M. Bolton, Edwin Butter, byvalet, Steve Collender, Destinyweddingstudio, Tsepova Ekaterina, Brian Gerber, Hajakely, Arto Hakola, Victoria Hillman, Monika Hrdinova, Roland IJdema, Anton_Ivanov, Pavel Kovacs, kungverylucky, Dudarev Mikhail, Marcella Miriello, Damian Ryszawy, Paul Schuster, Shiler, Stanislav Solovkin)

Library of Congress Cataloging-in-Publication Data
Names: Gish, Melissa, author.
Title: Lemurs / Melissa Gish.
Series: Living wild.
Includes bibliographical references and index.
Summary: A look at lemurs, including their habitats, physical characteristics such as their dexterous fingers and toes, behaviors, relationships with humans, and their threatened island habitat in the world today.
Identifiers: LCCN 2016036681 / ISBN 978-1-60818-830-7 (hardcover) / ISBN 978-1-62832-433-4 (pbk) / ISBN 978-1-56660-878-7 (eBook)
Subjects: LCSH: Lemurs—Juvenile literature.
Classification: LCC QL737.P9 G567 2017 / DDC 599.8/3—dc23

CCSS: RI.5.1, 2, 3, 8; RST.6-8.1, 2, 5, 6, 8; RH.6-8.3, 4, 5, 6, 7, 8

First Edition HC 9 8 7 6 5 4 3 2 1
First Edition PBK 9 8 7 6 5 4 3 2 1

CREATIVE EDUCATION • CREATIVE PAPERBACKS

LEMURS

Melissa Gish

A ghostly wail echoes through the trees in Madagascar's Anjanaharibe-Sud Reserve.

It is the cry of an indri, the world's largest lemur.

A ghostly wail echoes through the trees in Madagascar's Anjanaharibe-Sud Reserve. It is the cry of an indri, the world's largest lemur. Its call is met with a distant reply, and then several more. The chorus of siren-like sounds soon fills the forest. The family group must stay in close contact, for danger lurks below on the forest floor. Suddenly, the sound of the conversation changes. The calls become

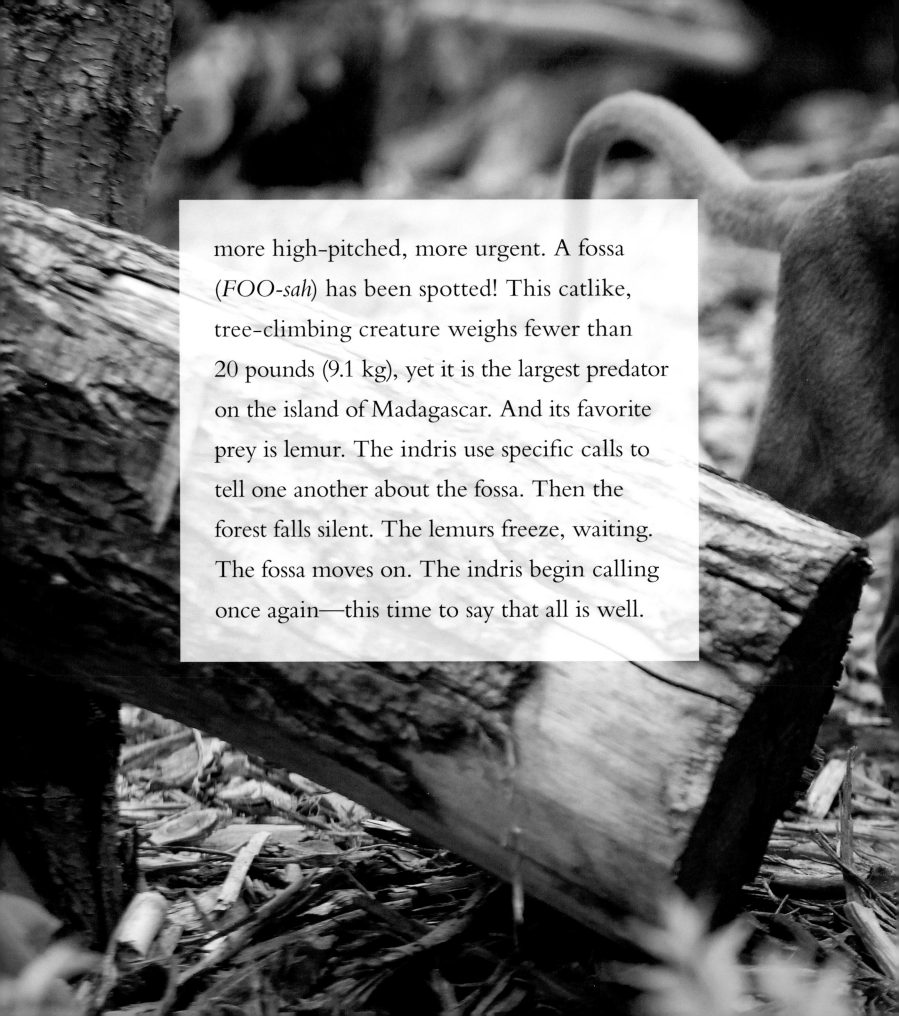

more high-pitched, more urgent. A fossa
(*FOO-sah*) has been spotted! This catlike,
tree-climbing creature weighs fewer than
20 pounds (9.1 kg), yet it is the largest predator
on the island of Madagascar. And its favorite
prey is lemur. The indris use specific calls to
tell one another about the fossa. Then the
forest falls silent. The lemurs freeze, waiting.
The fossa moves on. The indris begin calling
once again—this time to say that all is well.

WHERE IN THE WORLD THEY LIVE

■ **Brown Mouse Lemur**
southeastern Madagascar

■ **Fat-tailed Dwarf Lemur**
western Madagascar

■ **Red-tailed Sportive Lemur**
western Madagascar

■ **Diademed Sifaka**
northeastern Madagascar

■ **Aye-aye**
coastal Madagascar

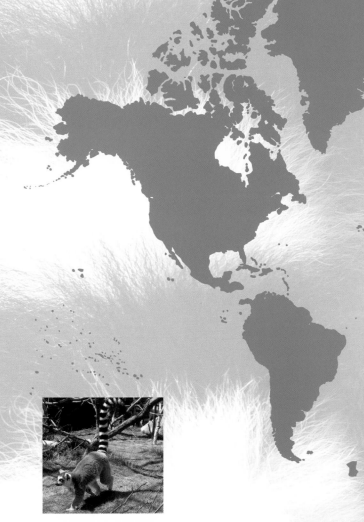

■ **Ring-tailed Lemur**
southwestern Madagascar

More than 100 lemur species can be found in Madagascar. The most endangered mammals in the world, these tree-dwelling primates live throughout the island's forests. Harboring rare woods that are in high demand around the world, Madagascar's forests are being rapidly depleted. As their woodland habitats shrink, lemur populations continue to decline. The colored squares represent the areas where six lemur species exist in the wild today.

LEAPIN' LEMURS

Lemurs are some of the oldest **mammals** on the planet and are included in the **primate** group prosimian, which means pre-monkey. The first lemur ancestors existed more than 70 million years ago in eastern Africa. They were mouse-sized and shared the world with dinosaurs. When mass **extinction** claimed the dinosaurs and most other large animals, the tiny lemurs survived. A few million years later, some of them made their way to the island of Madagascar. There they flourished. In the meantime, lemurs continued living on the African continent, along with their closest prosimian relatives, bushbabies, lorises, and pottos. But when monkeys emerged roughly 20 million years ago, they competed fiercely with lemurs for resources. While most prosimians became nocturnal (active at night), and turned to eating insects to avoid competition with herbivorous monkeys, lemurs were driven to extinction on the African continent. The lemurs in Madagascar, however—with few predators and little competition for resources—thrived and developed into the myriad species that exist today.

Mongoose lemurs are cathemeral, or active at varying times, day and night, throughout the year.

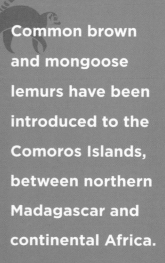

Common brown and mongoose lemurs have been introduced to the Comoros Islands, between northern Madagascar and continental Africa.

Nearly 30 species make up the family of sportive lemurs, which are also known as weasel lemurs.

Woolly lemurs are so named because their fur is short and woolly rather than long and silky, like that of their cousins.

Currently, more than 100 different lemurs are divided into 5 families. To reduce competition for food, some lemurs are nocturnal, while others are diurnal, or active during the day. Mouse and dwarf lemurs are the smallest—some weigh only an ounce (28.3 g). Sportive lemurs can weigh up to two pounds (0.9 kg). Both of these groups are nocturnal. True lemurs include ring-tailed, ruffed, bamboo, and numerous other species. They vary from 3 to 10 pounds (1.4–4.5 kg). The family of woolly lemurs also includes nine sifaka (*shee-FAHK*) species and the indri. These are the largest living lemurs, with some weighing more than 20 pounds (9.1 kg). True and woolly lemurs are diurnal. The three-foot-long (0.9 m) aye-aye is the only member of its family, and it is the world's largest nocturnal primate. At least 17 additional lemur species went extinct between 2,000 and 500 years ago, when humans began inhabiting Madagascar. These were the largest lemurs, with some species weighing more than 400 pounds (181 kg)—the size of a gorilla. The most endangered primates on the planet, every lemur species alive today faces the threat of extinction.

Lemurs are primarily arboreal, meaning they live mostly in trees, and their anatomy is suited to this lifestyle.

Coquerel's sifakas spend up to 40 percent of the day foraging, relying on about 12 different plant species for nourishment.

Lemurs have nimble fingers and toes, but unlike some of their primate relatives, they cannot grip with their tails.

They have slender bodies with long arms and legs. Lemurs have five fingers on each hand and five toes on each foot. Their first digit is spread far from the others, like a thumb. This allows lemurs to grip with both their hands and feet. The bottoms of the hands and feet are covered with a thick, leathery skin that helps lemurs get a firm grip on everything from tree trunks to vertical cliffs. Their fingers and toes are **dexterous**, allowing lemurs to pick at food, groom their fur, and hold small objects. Lemurs' digits have nails on all but the second toe, which has a thick claw used for grooming and scratching.

Most lemurs do not swim, but there is one exception. Weighing about two and a half pounds (1.1 kg), the Lac Alaotra bamboo lemur hides among the dense reed beds on the shore of Lake Alaotra. Some lemurs, such as ring-tailed lemurs, forage on the forest floor. Their arms and legs are about the same length, so they can run on all fours. Other species live almost exclusively in trees. Their hind legs are as much as 35 percent longer than their arms. To travel across the ground, which they rarely do, leaping lemurs must bound on their hind legs in a behavior called a dance-hop. Usually lemurs move from

Like most lemurs, the ring-tailed lemur does not swim, instead admiring Madagascar's many rivers from a safe distance.

Lemurs have four to six long bottom teeth set close together like a comb, which is why they are called the toothcomb.

tree to tree by leaping vertically and clinging to trunks. Muscular back legs catapult them through the air as they travel through the forest in this manner.

Lemurs are sometimes confused with monkeys. Although the two primates are related, they are very different. Monkeys have long, **prehensile** tails, but lemurs use their tails only for balance. Sifakas and indris have short tails, while most other lemurs have long tails—some as long as their bodies. In addition, studies have shown that lemurs are smarter than monkeys in many ways. At the Duke University Lemur Center in North Carolina, lemurs have revealed the ability to detect and repeat patterns and to understand simple math concepts.

The 18th-century Swedish **botanist** and **zoologist** Carolus Linnaeus is credited with giving many of the plants and animals of the world the names by which they are known today. After traveling to Madagascar, he wrote, "I call them lemurs, because they go around mainly by night, in a certain way similar to humans, and roam with a slow pace." Linnaeus named the leaping primates after creatures from Roman **mythology** called *lemures*, which were wandering spirits of the dead.

Although they are agile climbers (and leapers), ring-tailed lemurs spend a third of their time on the ground.

Fat-tailed dwarf lemurs help their forest habitats grow by pollinating trees and dispersing seeds.

Though not all lemurs are nocturnal, the smallest lemurs survive by hiding away during daylight hours. Mouse and dwarf lemurs hunt only at night, and, uniquely among primates, these types have the ability to go long periods without food or water. From about May to October, when food is scarce, these lemurs can enter a state of torpor, which is a kind of temporary hibernation in which body systems slow down and the animals sleep. Mouse and dwarf lemurs forage alone, but when they sleep during the day, and during torpor, a dozen or more of them will bunch together in holes in trees. These groups are called lemur balls.

Lemurs have large eyes, but their vision is not strong. They lack the light-sensitive cells necessary to see sharp details and colors. Diurnal lemurs can see yellow and blue colors but cannot distinguish between red and green. Nocturnal lemurs see only in shades of black. Lemurs' eyes are equipped with a reflective layer of tissue called the tapetum lucidum. This tissue collects light and centers it in the **retina**, helping nocturnal lemurs see movement in dim light. The tissue also causes eyeshine, making the eyes reflect color when light is shined on them. Lemurs' eyeshine varies by species and includes white, yellow, orange, and red colors.

Like all nocturnal lemurs, sportive lemurs must hide from predatory animals when they sleep during the day.

Mouse and dwarf lemurs store extra fat in their tails from which they draw nutrition during torpor.

Though most troops consist of males, females, and pups, some drive out the males to live alone or form all-male groups.

FRIENDS AND FAMILY

A group of lemurs is called a conspiracy or a troop, but not all lemurs live in groups. Nocturnal lemurs are generally solitary. They may nest and sleep in groups, but upon waking, they scatter and forage individually. Diurnal lemurs tend to be more social. The indri stays in family groups of 2 to 6 members, and sifaka troops may include up to 10 members. Ring-tailed lemurs, the most social species, live in conspiracies containing as many as 25 members. Lemur troops are organized by a strict **hierarchy** and led by a dominant female, called the matriarch. Usually the oldest, she decides where the group goes and what the members eat. The best food goes to the higher-ranking members. Every lemur knows its place in the group. Males rank lowest in a lemur troop. Even low-ranking females have more power than males in the group.

Troops tend to stay in a particular territory where they know food is available. The size of the territory, called a home range, varies by species. The common brown lemur's home range may be less than 2 acres (0.8 ha), while the Coquerel's sifaka may roam 10 to 22 acres

Aye-ayes' teeth never stop growing, so the lemurs must frequently chew wood to keep their teeth in check.

More than twice the size of the aye-aye, the giant aye-aye was also nocturnal but died out about 1,000 years ago.

(4–8.9 ha). A collared brown lemur group may claim up to 50 acres (20.2 ha), and the red-ruffed lemur's home range could extend to 150 acres (60.7 ha). Home ranges are determined by the availability of food in relation to the size of a family group.

Lemurs' diets vary greatly by species. Mouse and dwarf lemurs are voracious predators of frogs, baby birds, and insects. Most other lemurs are generally herbivores, meaning they eat plants, fruits, and nuts. Some species, such as the ring-tailed lemur, add spiders and insects to their diet. Black lemurs eat millipedes, which contain a **toxin** that makes most other animals sick. Other species, such as the Bemaraha woolly lemur, are strict vegetarians and will not eat any living creatures.

Some lemurs have highly specialized diets. Sifakas are folivores, meaning they eat mostly leaves and plant stems. The podlike fruit of the tamarind tree makes up most of the red-fronted brown lemur's diet. And bamboo lemurs are named for the woody plants they eat—plants that are deadly to other animals because they contain cyanide. Bamboo lemurs are immune to this poison and regularly eat about 12 times the amount that would kill most other

animals their size. The aye-aye eats nuts, palm tree nectar, certain fungi, and insect **larvae** that bore tunnels in trees. To get the larvae, the aye-aye taps trees with its extra-long middle finger. It listens for the sound of movement under the bark. Detecting a larva, the aye-aye uses its sharp front teeth to remove the bark and reveal the larva's tunnel. The aye-aye then sticks its middle finger into the tunnel. The sharply curved nail hooks the larva and pulls it out to be devoured.

Ruffed lemurs are the only diurnal primates to keep their newborns in nests, which they build in treetops.

The indri's call has a three-part pattern of an opening roar, a long note, and then a high-pitched finish.

Lemurs establish the boundaries of their feeding grounds by scent marking. **Glands** on their wrists, elbows, neck, and reproductive region emit musk, a greasy substance with an odor specific to each animal. Lemurs rub this musk on trees and rocks. They may also use urine or saliva to let other lemur groups know that the area is occupied. Lemurs' home ranges may overlap, but as long as food is not scarce, lemur groups—even different species—tend to get along. Scent recognition is also how family members keep from straying too far away from one another. More often, however, lemurs vocalize to stay in touch.

Most lemurs are highly vocal. Mothers typically purr to their offspring. Other sounds include growling, grunting, yowling, and mewing like a cat. Family members call to each other using a series of tones or a pitch unique to the family. Alarm calls, which are generally understood by all lemurs, regardless of species, let lemurs know when danger is near. Lemurs even have different calls for various predators, such as the Madagascar harrier hawk and the fossa. Small lemurs, such as the hairy-eared dwarf lemur, squeak their alarm,

Ring-tailed lemurs eat a variety of leaves, flowers, tree bark, and sap, but their main source of nutrition is fruit.

Many of Madagascar's snakes prey on lemurs, though none of them is venomous, instead killing prey by squeezing it to death.

while ring-tailed lemurs scream. The red-ruffed lemur's cry can be heard more than half a mile (0.8 km) away, and the wailing, trumpet-like call of the indri can reach more than a mile (1.6 km) through the forest.

Lemurs also call out to signal to one another that the time has come for mating. The mating season begins after the end of the rainy season, in April, and lasts until about June. However, during this time, each female lemur is fertile for only a matter of hours. She must mate with as many males as possible in this short time in order to ensure pregnancy. The **gestation** period varies by species and ranges from 9 to 24 weeks. Sifakas and indris usually give birth to just one baby, called a pup. If food is plentiful, twins may occur. But if food is scarce, the pup may fail to develop inside the mother. Most other lemur species have litters of three pups on average. Several species of ruffed lemurs may have as many as six pups at a time, if conditions are favorable.

Most lemur pups clutch their mother's underside for the first two to four weeks of life, feeding on the nutritious milk she produces. Then they are carried on their mother's back, sampling the food she consumes. In this way, they

learn what is good to eat. By the time they are between four and six months old, young lemurs no longer need their mother's milk. In social species, females typically remain with their family group, while young males venture away to establish their own home ranges. When she is two or three years old, a female will join an unrelated male in his territory so that they can begin their own family group. Lemurs in the wild typically survive between 15 and 20 years. Kept in captivity, where the danger of predators is eliminated and food is abundant, lemurs have lived more than 30 years.

A ring-tailed lemur pup clings to its mother's stomach for about two weeks before moving to her upper back.

Scientists estimate that fewer than 10,000 indris remain in their native Madagascan habitat, and numbers keep declining.

FOLKLORE AND FADY

Lemurs are an integral part of the traditions of the **indigenous** Malagasy people of Madagascar. The mythology of the Tanala **ethnic** group in southeastern Madagascar includes a story that explains the relationship between lemurs and humans. An innocent man was accused of a crime. He fled into the forest, and his accusers chased him. To save the man, the spirits of the forest transformed him into an indri. He became the founder of a new race—the lemurs. The indri was called *babakoto*, which means "grandfather," and he was the most respected of all the lemurs.

Another Tanala story explains why it is *fady* (a Malagasy word meaning "forbidden") to kill the indri. One day, a man was working in the forest. He climbed a rubber tree and began to tap a hole to extract the rubber. Suddenly, he slipped and fell. Just as he was about to hit the ground, babakoto leaped from a nearby tree and caught him. The man was so grateful that he told his people to never harm babakoto. Among many ethnic groups in Madagascar, this custom still exists. While other cultures have influenced traditional Malagasy beliefs

Most of the people who live in Madagascar continue to lead a traditional lifestyle based on agriculture.

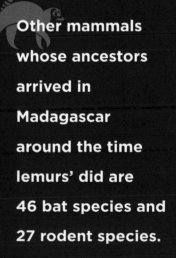

Other mammals whose ancestors arrived in Madagascar around the time lemurs' did are 46 bat species and 27 rodent species.

Sifaka *is a Malagasy name that was given to the lemur group for its distinctive call, which sounds like* shif-AUK.

To stay in touch with its family group, a silky sifaka makes an average of seven calls every hour while foraging.

in recent decades, for many native people, harming an indri is still fady.

The neighboring Betsimisaraka people believe that lemurs are the ancestors of humans. A long time ago, the mysterious aye-aye had two sons. At night, the sons hunted insects and gathered nuts. They slept in the trees during the day. One of the sons grew tired of this lifestyle and decided to leave the forest. "I want to grow my own food," he said. "And I want to live in the sunlight." And so he went to the flatland and grew crops. His children—descendants of the aye-aye—became the first humans. The other son stayed behind and created many more lemurs to fill the forest. Even today, the Betsimisaraka people respect aye-ayes as their ancestors. If they find a dead aye-aye, they hold a funeral and bury it, just as they would a person.

Not all Malagasy people treat the aye-aye with such respect. Because of the aye-aye's strange features, many ethnic groups view it as a demon. One tradition holds that an aye-aye looking at a person with its yellow eyes will cause the person to become sick, and an aye-aye pointing its long middle finger at someone means certain death for that person. Aye-ayes are not fearful of humans,

so they sometimes wander into villages. Because of the dread associated with aye-ayes, villagers will kill the animals on sight. Some scholars believe the name aye-aye is derived from the Malagasy phrase *heh heh*, which means, "I don't know"—a term referring to the creature so feared that the people never speak its name.

A name that became popular at the end of the 1990s was Zoboomafoo. Known from the television show by the same name, this Coquerel's sifaka leaped onto the scene in January 1999. *Zoboomafoo*, which ran through November 2001, was a spin-off from the show *Kratts' Creatures*. Both shows were created and hosted by brothers

Most aye-ayes are found along the eastern third of Madagascar, emerging from their leafy nests at night to forage.

REMEMBERING JOVIAN

For the Duke Lemur Center, the death of Jovian—a Coquerel's sifaka who called the center home for 20 years—meant the loss of a lemur praised for his kindness and spirit. But for teenagers and twenty-somethings across the country, it meant the loss of a childhood icon—Zoboomafoo, the titular role Jovian played on the popular kids TV show.

Footage of Jovian was a centerpiece of the popular wildlife show, which aired 65 episodes from 1999 to 2001, and is still syndicated. The much-loved lemur died of kidney failure [November 10, 2014] at the age of 20, leaving behind a legacy as a playful friend and caring father, in addition to a television star....

"He was funny," [Martin] Kratt said, recalling how Jovian would grab his hair or nose while filming. "There was a lot of great interaction, and it made for a lot of great moments."

Outside of the show, Jovian was described as a "capable and caring father," who sired 12 sifakas by two different partners, leading to four grandbabies and two on the way, according to the center's website.

From Duke University's The Chronicle, *November 12, 2014*

Chris and Martin Kratt. Chris earned a degree in biology, and Martin graduated from Duke University in North Carolina with a degree in zoology. While in college, Martin worked at the Duke Lemur Center, a research and **captive-breeding** facility. When Chris and Martin needed an animal to help host their new show, they decided to feature a lemur from Duke University.

In real life, Zoboomafoo was a Coquerel's sifaka named Jovian, who was born at the center in 1994. A set was built at the center, and parts of the Kratts' show were filmed in one of the lemur enclosures. Zoboomafoo would jump through the window, and the Kratt brothers would feed him mangos or garbanzo beans as a treat. Then he would magically turn into a talking lemur. In reality, he was replaced by a puppet for this part of the show. The popularity of Zoboomafoo brought awareness to the plight of lemurs and greatly increased the number of visitors to the Duke Lemur Center. Jovian lived to be nearly 21 years old. His children and grandchildren are part of the captive-breeding program at the Duke Lemur Center.

In May 2015, twin ring-tailed lemur pups were born at the Duke Lemur Center. The female pups were named

Duke University has successfully bred black-and-white ruffed lemurs and released them in Madagascar's Betampona Nature Reserve.

Research has shown that captive ring-tailed lemurs are less active than wild lemurs.

Scientists with Nebraska's Henry Doorly Zoo & Aquarium have discovered more than 20 new lemur species in Madagascar since 1999.

Princess Julien I and Princess Julien II in honor of King Julien, the self-proclaimed lemur leader featured in the *Madagascar* movie series from DreamWorks Pictures. King Julien first appeared in *Madagascar* (2005) as a hyperactive, loudmouthed ring-tailed lemur that loved to dance. He showed up again in *Madagascar: Escape 2 Africa* (2008), *Madagascar 3: Europe's Most Wanted* (2012), and *Penguins of Madagascar* (2014). In addition, he has appeared in several direct-to-video movies and video games, and in 2014, Netflix launched the television show *All Hail King Julien.* The show takes place in the years before the first Madagascar movie, when Julien first becomes king of the lemurs. His party-all-the-time attitude often gets him into trouble while his nemesis, Karl the fanaloka (a small catlike relative of the fossa), constantly plots against him.

Real-life ring-tailed lemurs get into nearly as much trouble in the 3D documentary *Island of Lemurs: Madagascar* (2014), from Warner Bros. and IMAX Entertainment. The movie features many kinds of lemurs, including a troop of ring-tailed lemurs that sometimes sneaks onto nearby farms to raid crops. The 2005 PBS documentary *A Lemur's Tale* follows a group of baby ring-tailed lemurs on their perilous

Although Maurice the aye-aye often has little confidence in King Julien's plans, he nevertheless follows his leader.

path from birth to adulthood. The popular ring-tailed lemur even has its own breakfast cereal. Leapin' Lemurs is an organic, gluten-free cereal from EnviroKidz. The company donates a portion of its profits to animal research, including the Lemur Conservation Foundation (LCF) in Myakka City, Florida. In 2012, Leapin' Lemurs also helped fund the publication of a six-book series by the LCF. The series consists of *Ako the Aye-aye, Bitika the Mouse Lemur, Tik-Tik the Ring-tailed Lemur, Bounce the White Sifaka, Furry and Fuzzy the Red-Ruffed Lemur Twins*, and *No-Song the Indri*.

The blue-eyed black lemur is also called Sclater's lemur for British zoologist Philip Sclater, who wrote about it in 1864.

EARTH'S MOST ENDANGERED MAMMALS

Deforestation is the greatest threat to not only lemurs but also many other plant and animal species around the world.

Lemurs share their island home with more than 8,000 species of plants and animals, most of which are also **endemic** to Madagascar, and many of which are threatened by human activities. In 2012, the International Union for Conservation of Nature (IUCN) named lemurs the most endangered mammals on Earth. Lemurs are in trouble mainly because of hunting and habitat loss. The growing human population of Madagascar, combined with widespread poverty, has increased the need for cheap food. Despite many species being protected by law, lemurs are routinely hunted for food. Logging of precious rosewood, ebony, and other rare hardwoods has caused massive deforestation. Government bans on logging in national parks are ineffective because there are too few law enforcement officers to patrol the forests. Birds, amphibians, and especially lemurs suffer the loss of trees and plants vital to their survival. Likewise, the construction of mines that produce gemstones, copper, iron, and gold destroy critical habitats.

The lemurs' greatest threat is something that has been ongoing since humans first arrived on the island 2,000

Widespread poverty forces many rural Malagasy people to get by without up-to-date equipment.

Most lemurs get the moisture they need from food; some species, such as the greater bamboo lemur, drink no water at all.

years ago: *tavy*, or slash-and-burn agriculture. Tavy is mostly used for converting forests into rice fields. An area of forest is cut, burned, and then planted with rice. After a year or two, the ground becomes less fertile, so a new area is cut and burned. The forest never grows back. Instead, weeds and low bushes grow, leaving the land vulnerable to wildfires. The slash-and-burn method is also used to clear land for cattle pastures. When people first came to Madagascar, they brought with them animals called zebu. These humpbacked cattle drink little water and withstand heat better than other types of cattle. There are now more zebu on Madagascar than there are people.

Humans have destroyed more than 90 percent of the island's forests for logging, farming, and grazing. Lemurs have been pushed into small, **fragmented** pockets of forest and marshland. Cut off from others of their kind, lemur populations continue to decline, and some have already gone extinct. One species, the greater bamboo lemur, was not spotted for many years. It was considered extinct—that is, until **primatologist** Dr. Patricia Wright rediscovered a few of them in 1986. She also discovered a new species, the golden bamboo lemur. Both are critically

Bamboo lemurs constitute the genus Hapalemur, whose name derives from the Greek word hapalos, or "gentle."

The mountains of Ranomafana National Park are very steep, which helps protect the region from illegal logging that occurs elsewhere.

endangered, and Dr. Wright, a professor of **anthropology** at Stony Brook University in New York, has worked extensively to protect them. She helped establish Ranomafana National Park in eastern Madagascar—home to a variety of bamboo lemurs. Like many other lemurs, bamboo lemurs' specialized diet limits their ability to seek out new territories when their primary food has been destroyed, often resulting in starvation.

One lemur species that seems to be doing better than all the others is the ring-tailed lemur. While still in danger of extinction, the ring-tailed lemur has demonstrated the ability to adapt to an environment shared with humans. Unlike lemurs that rely on specialized diets, ring-tails have adopted an omnivorous diet, which means they eat both animals and plants. Such flexibility has allowed ring-tails to survive as easily near villages and farms as they do deep in forests. But even ring-tails have limited survival abilities. Dr. Michelle Sauther of the University of Colorado Boulder studies ring-tailed lemurs to find out what these limits are and how the lemurs might survive as their environment continues to change. Visitors to the University of Colorado website can read about the Beza Mahafaly Lemur Biology Project, which is named for the nature reserve in southern Madagascar where the lemurs are studied. Dr. Sauther's work is featured in the American Museum of Natural History's film *Lemurs of Madagascar— Surviving on an Island of Change*, which can be viewed on YouTube.

In October 2014, a group of researchers led by Dr. Alfred Rosenberger, an anthropologist at Brooklyn College in New York, went on a lemur hunt. This was no ordinary expedition, though. They went to investigate a series of flooded freshwater caves in Tsimanampetsotsa National Park in southwestern Madagascar in hopes of finding the remains of ancient animals. A team of scuba

The critically endangered diademed sifaka is named for the fur around its head, which looks like a diadem, or crown.

Sifakas spend almost 20 percent of the day playing with and grooming each other, which strengthens family bonds.

divers led by Phillip Lehman of the Dominican Republic **Speleological** Society explored the caves. They found hundreds of **subfossils** of extinct lemurs in one of the caves. Along with the lemur subfossils, the remains of extinct elephant birds, early turtles and crocodiles, and other ancient animals were found. Some of the lemur remains include those of *Pachylemur*, or the giant ruffed lemur. Despite bearing a close resemblance to modern ruffed lemurs, this extinct creature weighed about 36 pounds (16.3 kg)—roughly 4 times the size of modern ruffed lemurs. Subfossils of *Mesopropithecus* were also found. This was a sloth-lemur, so named for the way it moved through the trees like a sloth, hanging upside down and pulling itself hand-over-hand along branches, rather than leaping like most lemurs today. *Mesopropithecus* weighed about the same as *Pachylemur*. Dr. Rosenberger's team hopes to learn more about lemur evolution by conducting **DNA** tests on the subfossils.

DNA is a vital tool in the study of evolution. In 2008, scientists at Duke University were able to use DNA to map the lemur genome, meaning they traced the branches of the lemur family tree. Their work revealed that of the five

basic types of lemurs, the aye-aye was the first to branch off from a common lemur ancestor about 66 million years ago, making the aye-aye the oldest lemur—and perhaps the oldest primate—on the planet. By understanding where lemurs came from, scientists and conservationists hope to better understand where the animals are headed in the future. Madagascar's environment has reached a critical point of overuse, and lemurs have no chance of survival without help from their human neighbors and scientists alike. Without earnest efforts to stop the destruction of their forests, the people of Madagascar will no longer be able to call their home the island of lemurs.

Lemurs have 18 to 36 teeth, with larger species having the most and smaller species having fewer.

ANIMAL TALE: CROCODILE AND THE LEMURS

The wildlife of Madagascar is tightly woven into the fabric of the Malagasy people's culture. Stories that contribute to the island's mythology are called *tafasiry*, and many explain how things came to be. The following tafasiry from the northern region of Madagascar tells why some animals look the way they do.

Long ago, Croco Mada, the crocodile who spent his days swimming in the river and sunning himself on the riverbank, grew bored of eating fish. He decided to visit the forest, a place he had never been before. Dragging his heavy tail behind him, Croco Mada climbed up over the riverbank and entered the lush forest.

Papango, the hawk, watched Croco Mada from his perch high above the forest floor. He knew from experience that wherever Croco Mada went, trouble followed. "Are you lost?" Papango called. Croco Mada looked up and spied the bird. "The river is that way," Papango said, pointing east.

"I am not lost," Croco Mada replied, and he continued walking. Soon he came upon Tsipoy, the partridge. *What a tasty snack*, Croco Mada thought to himself. He crept ever so quietly toward Tsipoy and slowly opened his mouth.

Just as Croco Mada was about to devour Tsipoy, Papango cried from above, "Watch out!" Croco Mada snapped his jaws shut, but Tsipoy flapped his wings and escaped with only a scratch on his breast. This is why the partridge, to this day, has a red spot on his breast.

Croco Mada would not give up so easily. He continued deeper into the forest. Soon he came upon Babakoto, who was busy chewing seeds from the center of a fruit. Croco Mada silently crept up behind Babakoto and opened his mouth. *You will taste very good*, Croco Mada thought to himself.

But just as before, Papango cried, "Watch out!" at the very moment Croco Mada snapped his jaws shut. Babakoto leaped forward just in time. Although he managed to escape death, Babakoto lost his tail to Croco Mada, who swallowed it in one quick gulp. This is why the indri, to this day, has only a stub tail.

Croco Mada was growing weary. He decided that instead of hunting he would lie down and set a trap. And so he covered himself with leaves, put some delicious palm seeds on his tongue, and waited with his jaws wide open. Before long, Aye-aye came along and, spying the palm seeds, reached eagerly for them with both hands.

"Watch out!" came Papango's warning. Aye-aye pulled back his hands, but he wasn't quick enough. His middle fingers were caught in Croco Mada's jaws. Aye-aye pulled and pulled, and finally he freed his fingers. They were stretched to twice the length of his other fingers, but he escaped with his life. This is why the aye-aye, to this day, has long middle fingers.

Croco Mada glared up at Papango and shouted, "Why do you spoil everything?"

Papango looked Croco Mada square in the eyes. "Because I am the hunter in the forest, and you don't belong here." Then Papango pointed to the east again. "The river is that way."

Croco Mada realized that Papango was right, so he went back to the river. And that is why the crocodile, to this day, does not hunt in the forest.

GLOSSARY

anthropology – the study of the history of humankind

botanist – a scientist who studies plants and their growth

captive-breeding – being bred and raised in a place from which escape is not possible

dexterous – having the skill or agility to use the hands or body to perform tasks

DNA – deoxyribonucleic acid; a substance found in every living thing that determines the species and individual characteristics of that thing

endemic – native to and confined to a certain geographical location

ethnic – sharing distinctive cultural traits as a group in society

extinction – the act or process of becoming extinct; coming to an end or dying out

fragmented – a habitat that has been broken up into scattered sections that may result in difficulty moving safely from one place to another

gestation – the period of time it takes a baby to develop inside its mother's womb

glands – organs in a human or animal body that produce chemical substances used by other parts of the body

hierarchy – a system in which people, animals, or things are ranked in importance one above another

indigenous – originating in a particular region or country

larvae – the newly hatched, wingless, often wormlike form of many insects before they become adults

mammals – warm-blooded animals that have a backbone and hair or fur, give birth to live young, and produce milk to feed their young

mythology – a collection of myths, or popular, traditional beliefs or stories that explain how something came to be or that are associated with a person or object

prehensile – capable of grasping

primate – a mammal with a large brain and gripping hands; lemurs, monkeys, apes, and humans are primates

primatologist – a scientist who studies primates

retina – a layer or lining in the back of the eye that is sensitive to light

speleological – having to do with the exploration and scientific study of caves, sinkholes, underground streams, and caverns

subfossils – the remains of animals that have not become completely fossilized, or turned to rock

toxin – a substance that is harmful or poisonous

zoologist – a person who studies animals and their lives

SELECTED BIBLIOGRAPHY

Duke Lemur Center. "Research Areas." Duke University. http://lemur.duke.edu/discover/research-areas.

Fellman, Drew. *Island of Lemurs: Madagascar.* DVD. Directed by David Douglas. Burbank, Calif.: Warner Bros., 2014.

Mittermeier, Russell A., et al. *Lemurs of Madagascar.* 3rd ed. Arlington, Va.: Conservation International, 2010.

O'Neil, Dennis. "Lemurs." Palomar College. http://anthro.palomar.edu/primate/prim_2.htm.

San Diego Zoo Animals & Plants. "Lemur." http://animals.sandiegozoo.org/animals/lemur.

Wright, Patricia Chapple. *For the Love of Lemurs: My Life in the Wilds of Madagascar.* New York: Lantern Books, 2014.

Note: Every effort has been made to ensure that any websites listed above were active at the time of publication. However, because of the nature of the Internet, it is impossible to guarantee that these sites will remain active indefinitely or that their contents will not be altered.

As the most-threatened mammals on the planet, lemurs need humans' help if they are to survive in their native habitats.

INDEX